W9-AYO-652

Winter Carnivals
Festivals in White

Lisa Gabbert

The Rosen Publishing Group's
PowerKids Press ™
New York

To Mom, for all the footwork.

Published in 1999 by The Rosen Publishing Group, Inc.
29 East 21st Street, New York, NY 10010

First Edition

Book Design: Michael de Guzman

Photo Credits: p. 4 © Steve Bly/International Stock; p. 7 © Tony Demin/International Stock; p. 8 © I. Robert Stottlemyer/International Stock; p. 11 © Kirk Anderson/International Stock; p. 12 © Bob Firth/ International Stock; p. 15 © Frank Grant/International Stock; p. 16 © Bill Tucker/International Stock; p. 19 © Eric Sanford/International Stock; p. 20 © George Ancona/International Stock.

Gabbert, Lisa.
    Winter carnivals: festivals in white/ by Lisa Gabbert.
        p.   cm. — (Festivals! USA)
    Includes index.
    Summary: Describes the origin of the winter carnival held in McCall, Idaho, and tells what goes on there.
    ISBN 0-8239-5338-6
    1. Carnival—Idaho—McCall—Juvenile literature. 2. Winter festivals—Idaho—McCall—Juvenile literature. 3. McCall (Idaho)—Social life and customs—Juvenile literature. [1. Winter festivals. 2. Festivals. 3. McCall (Idaho)] I. Title. II. Series: Gabbert, Lisa. Festivals! USA.
    GT4211.M33G33 1998
    394.25—dc21   98-24015
                                                                                           CIP
                                                                                            AC

Manufactured in the United States of America

Contents

The Rocky Mountains

The Rocky Mountains make up a huge mountain **range** (RAYNJ) that runs through the western United States. This area is full of lakes, rivers, and forests. Winters in the Rockies are long and snowy.

McCall is a small town in central Idaho, right in the middle of the Northern Rockies. McCall is surrounded by forests and has its own lake. It is also one place for a winter carnival that has been enjoyed by people for more than 50 years.

◀ *Idaho is surrounded by beautiful mountains.*

Early Winter Carnivals

The first McCall winter carnival was in 1924. It was held because Idaho winters can be long and hard. Something had to be done to raise the spirits of the McCall people.

A railroad had been built to connect McCall to other cities. This train brought 248 people to the carnival, including the state **governor** (GUH-vern-er). The carnival held skiing **competitions** (kom-peh-TIH-shunz), as well as snowshoeing, dogsled races, and **skijoring** (skee-JOHR-ing).

Snowshoeing is just one of the competitions that still goes on at winter carnivals around the United States. ▶

Ice-out and Break-up Contests

Another part of the early winter carnivals were the ice-out and break-up contests.

Everyone wondered when the snow and ice would melt and spring would arrive. The people of McCall bet on when the ice would break up on the lake. A barrel was placed in the middle of the lake. A wire was hooked up from the barrel to a clock across the ice. When the connection broke between the barrel and the clock, the ice had broken.

Today, people try to guess when the barrel will touch the shore.

◄ *A frozen lake is one sign that it's a very cold winter.*

Sharlie

The story of Sharlie has been around for a long time. Sharlie is the name of the monster who is believed to live in McCall's lake. Sharlie is friendly, but very shy. Some people say that Sharlie is a big fish that can't be caught. Others think that Sharlie is just a **legend** (LEH-jend). Whether or not she exists, Sharlie is an important part of the McCall winter carnival and McCall history.

Mysterious stories about huge creatures living in lakes have been around for many years. The mystery of Sharlie has ▶ *become part of the McCall winter carnival.*

The Ice Sculptures

With more than two feet of snow on the ground, **residents** (REH-zih-dentz) of McCall have plenty of snow for their ice **sculptures** (SKULP-cherz). Some of the sculptures are over twenty feet high! Sharlie is always there, along with Big Bird, dragons, castles, and dinosaurs. Anything can be made into an ice sculpture. There is even a mini–golf course in ice. Sometimes the **temperature** (TEMP-rah-chur) is too warm and the artists must add more and more snow so the sculptures don't melt.

◀ *Creating an ice sculpture of this size takes talent and patience.*

How Do You Make a Sculpture?

Building an ice sculpture takes a lot of work. People spend many weeks planning what they will create. Artists work in teams, because the job is often too big for one person. They work at night, when the temperature is cold and they don't have to **compete** (kum-PEET) with the sun. Many people support their sculptures from the inside with pipes. Others just start with a big block of ice and get to work!

Slush is the main building material when making the sculptures. It is used to pack shapes together. ▶

The Sculpture Contest

Ice sculptures at the McCall winter carnival are entered in a contest, which is the biggest event of the carnival. There are usually more than 60 entries, and they are judged in different categories. There are prizes for the best action sculpture, the funniest sculpture, and the best nature scene. There is also a prize for the best **maintained** (mayn-TAYND) sculpture, because sometimes the sculptures melt. Of course, there is also the grand prize. All the winners are given prize money.

◀ *Children get a chance to compete in the snowman-building contest at the winter carnival.*

17

Dogsled Races

Dogsled races are a popular winter event. A person stands upright in a **sledge** (SLEJ), which is pulled by a team of dogs called huskies. Huskies are strong and have thick fur to protect them against the cold. Dogsled teams are usually made up of many dogs. Three-mile races have only four dogs per team, but races over 25 miles long have many more dogs per team. The main race at the winter carnival is 35 miles long. There is also a shorter one just for kids.

The dogsled races are an event where teamwork is important. ▶

The Parade

The grand parade is an important part of the carnival. The parade has a Mardi Gras **theme** (THEEM) because the winter carnival is held during the time of Mardi Gras. People decorate their cars and there are prizes for the best floats. People on floats dress in costumes and throw Mardi Gras beads and candy to the crowd. The local rodeo queens are also there. Two senior citizens are chosen as the Lord and Lady of the Lake. Smokey the Bear also arrives on the scene. Sharlie is there, too, as a 100-foot Chinese dragon.

◄ *The winter carnival parade is a lot like the Mardi Gras parade that takes place yearly in New Orleans, Louisiana.*

Fun at the Carnival

The carnival lasts for ten days but it can be hard to do and see everything! There are crawfish and pancake dinners, as well as hayrides, dances, and fireworks. There are also skijoring **demonstrations** (deh-mun-STRAY-shunz). Sometimes people ski behind cars instead of horses!

Everybody in McCall goes to the winter carnival to enjoy the snow and to look forward to the coming of spring.

There may be a winter festival happening near you!

Dutch Winterfest, Holland, MI

King 5 Winterfest, Seattle, WA

Ski Rodeo, Winthrop, WA

Winter Carnival, Fairbanks, AL

Glossary

compete (kum-PEET) To try hard to win at something.

competition (kom-peh-TIH-shun) A contest.

demonstration (deh-mun-STRAY-shun) Showing people how to do something by acting it out.

governor (GUH-vern-er) A political leader in a state.

legend (LEH-jend) A story that has been handed down through generations and is believed to be true.

maintain (mayn-TAYN) To keep going.

range (RAYNJ) A row or line of mountains.

resident (REH-zih-dent) Someone who lives in a certain town or city.

sculpture (SKULP-cher) A figure that is carved or formed.

skijoring (skee-JOHR-ing) Skiing behind a horse or car.

sledge (SLEJ) A sled with runners.

temperature (TEMP-rah-chur) How hot or cold something is.

theme (THEEM) A subject or topic.

Index